The NH Jobs for America's Graduates Program at Manc
nered with Alicia Aho for three years. During this time,
to the Teens Empowered program and Alicia's unique Your Tree of Life Program. These programs strongly assisted many in recognizing and utilizing their full potential, encouraging students to transform their dreams into reality…including attending college.

—Chantel Vaillancourt, MEd, Guidance Counselor, Pinkerton Academy

YOUR TREE
of
LIFE

The Young Adult Version

ALICIA AHO
A Certified Professional Coach - Creator of Teens Empowered Coaching Program

Copyright © 2015 Alicia Aho
All rights reserved.
ISBN: 1493637789
ISBN-13: 9781493637782

To Carol & Steve!
So awesome to meet & grow our friendship.
Lots of love~
Alicia 6/1/18

Dedicated to my friends and family who have been
my cheerleaders along this path!
Of course, to the students who were integral in making this happen!
Kudos to you!

Enjoy the Journey!
Alicia Aho
6/4/2015

TABLE OF CONTENTS
The Branches of Your Tree

> *Without courage, all other virtues lose their meaning.*
>
> —Winston Churchill, Prime Minister of the United Kingdom from 1940-45 (During WWII and 1951-55.)

	Foreword	vii
	Preface	ix
	Introduction	xi
Chapter 1	My Family Tree	1
Chapter 2	Dream Big	7
Chapter 3	Be Yourself	11
Chapter 4	Your Circumstances Don't Define You	15
Chapter 5	Character and Self-Awareness	19
Chapter 6	Discovery	25
Chapter 7	Strengthen and name Your Roots	29

Chapter 8	Habits — Strengthening your Roots	35
Chapter 9	You Control Your Future	39
Chapter 10	Making Changes	43
Chapter 11	Find a Mentor or Two	47
Chapter 12	Surround Yourself with Trusted Friendships	51
Chapter 13	Use Resources to Help You Grow—Personally and Professionally	55
Chapter 14	Important Roots to Nurture as Well as Exploring New Branches	59
Chapter 15	What Are Your Passions? What Brings You Joy? What Will Bring the Blossoms out of Your Tree of Life?	63
Chapter 16	What Are Your Nonnegotiables?	67
Chapter 17	Education Is a Strong Root to Help Your Tree of Life Grow	71
Chapter 18	Playtime: Everyone Needs It—Your Tree of Life Needs It, Too, Like Water and Air	75
Chapter 19	Areas You'd Like to Improve to Strengthen Your Tree of Life	79
Chapter 20	Always Keep Growing	83
Chapter 21	Help Others Grow	87
Chapter 22	Enjoy the Fruit of Your Effort	91
Chapter 23	Flourish	95

FOREWORD

In her book, <u>Your Tree of Life,</u> Alicia puts forth a relatively simple premise, "Your circumstances do not determine the outcome of your life; your actions and attitudes do." This premise, while relatively simplistic, is much more difficult to put into a practical, clear, well defined, and usable guide to taking control of your life--Alicia has met this goal.

This is not a book about good ideas or a step-by-step recipe on how to live your life. Alicia has taken her own life's experiences and used them to guide the reader and her students in establishing a doable path to develop the habits and a focus to overcome destructive beliefs and behaviors.

Since the author can speak from her first hand, "been through it" life experiences, her expertise and guidance come through on every page. Her direct work with youth at schools has also helped her lay the foundation for this must have book for both youth and their parents, and for counselors of troubled youth.

Through her own experiences and the use of an undernourished tree analogy, Alicia brilliantly demonstrates and models for youngsters how they can take control over their own lives rather than allow external forces to supplant and crowd out the good that surrounds them.

FOREWORD

While the book was originally authored for teens, there are many lessons and stimulating points to help people of all ages. By exploring Your Tree of Life, those who are bedeviled by forces beyond their immediate control will find their own voice and ultimately their own path to success.
Mihran Keoseian
Former Principal, School Superintendent, and Currently Urban School Turn-A-Round Specialist

PREFACE

This book has been a labor of love for many years. As a "believer in them," regarding teenagers and young adults, I knew, somehow, I needed to have a strong say in their future. Fewer adults will need self-help books if as teens they read this one.

As a pretty simple person—meaning not so different from most people—I thought my ideas of coaching teens weren't novel ones. Much to my surprise, many people believed kids don't have goals and wouldn't be accountable to setting and achieving weekly goals. I knew differently.

So as I sit here today with experience as my teacher, I'll do my best to coach you—the youth of the world—and hopefully parents, too, so that you don't ever let your circumstances determine the outcome of your life. I'll make sure you believe that I know you'll be a success in all you're passionate about.

Thank you for reading this book. May it be an essential tool in Your Life's Toolbox.

INTRODUCTION

It is my hope that this book is a great tool for you to use to assist you on your journey during this time of your personal growth. This book is written as a process for you to read and journal/draw/take photographs and develop many ideas of your own as you grow each and every day. The intention is for you to read at least a chapter a week and participate in the personal work assigned in the chapter. As you can see, it is not a thick book, but it is full of ways that, if you follow the guidance, you will reap a lifetime of blessings. That is my hope.

What you need for Your Tree of Life program is a personal journal, or a Moleskine (leather bound notebook), you could also get a sketch book if that is a way you would like to express yourself. Also know, as you will see, that I do express myself in photographs. You may also discover photography may be an outlet for your creativity.

Most of all, give yourself time, space, and courage to go on this most important journey. It took a lot of courage for me to write this for you, but you are worth every single letter. Many blessings.

CHAPTER ONE

My Family Tree

When you envision a family tree, many of you will see a healthy tree with many branches, or perhaps you may see a literal family tree that has been written by hand with "branches" showing people's names and family titles, ie, paternal grandfather, maternal great grandmother, etc. My hope is this book and the work that you will do, as well as hearing the stories I will share, will help shine a light on your own family tree. My family tree is dying. The trunk of my family tree is addiction, and many of the branches are various forms of addiction:

- Alcoholism
- Drug addiction
- Pill addiction
- Addiction to chaos
- Food addiction
- Gambling addiction
- Nicotine addiction

Those branches of my family tree led to abusive, unhealthy behaviors. They grew far and wide on all sides of my family. Unhealthy behaviors were

MY FAMILY TREE

commonplace. I was a "straight-A" student and a talented musician. I played the violin, but it didn't matter. What mattered in my case was that I had to take care of my house and take responsibility for my own life because my family tree was rotting away—no one was nourishing it.

My undernourished Family Tree—and the results. However, this is not My Tree of Life.

What usually happens in family trees such as these is *people allow their circumstances to determine the outcomes of their lives.* Working with teens, I know many young people who are in this exact position. Many teenagers may not have the same experiences that I've had, but they have similar feelings, lack of confidence or courage to try things/classes that will help them in their own futures. Some will sacrifice their own futures to be the "caretakers" for their families. This needs to change.

YOUR TREE OF LIFE

When I describe my tree to you, it's for a reason, because trees are going to be a theme in this book and in Your Life's Toolbox. The great thing about trees is they're everywhere.

My family tree is sick and suffering, and many branches have died from addiction. But let's not forget that it's my *family* tree, not *my* tree! Let me say that again because that will be an analogy throughout this book: your *family* tree is not *your* tree.

You have your own tree—starting with fresh soil and roots—and it can grow up in any direction, into any type of tree you want. What kind of tree do you envision as yours:

- a crazy, curvy tree;
- a tall, straight, strong oak tree;
- a beautiful, flowering cherry blossom tree;
- a forsythia bush;
- a tall white birch;
- a pine tree;
- a sweet maple tree;
- a huge redwood—whoa;
- a giant sequoia; or
- a rose bush?

You can be any tree you want. It's *your* tree!

Working together, we'll explore your "land," the foundation for your tree, through a process of self-discovery. What are your interests and passions? These will grow strong roots. And what are those roots? It's your education, healthy people, and family growing a strong core, with strong foundations, establishing good habits, making great choices, developing integrity and philanthropy, flourishing, enjoying the rewards from all of your hard work, every day of your life.

So believe, as I do, that this simple process of self-awareness, personal reflection, and growth will provide you with a lifetime of blessings, and perhaps you won't need self-help books as an adult, because you created good habits and worked hard while you were young.

MY FAMILY TREE

Build up Your Life's Toolbox now. Start with this book. I'll give you other tools along your journey. Remember, my friend, I believe in the power of youth! *Your circumstances don't determine the outcome of your life; your actions and attitudes do.* I'll be here, cheering you on, showing you the way.

You see, at sixteen years old, I was *homeless*, but I found a way to graduate from high school with honors. (I was living in another city and sleeping on a friend's couch). I went to college and kept on pushing. It was hard, and I had roadblocks—big ones—but I believe my life was the way it was for a reason. It forced me to take responsibility for myself and change what I didn't like about my circumstances. Due to that hard work, now I'm a certified professional life coach, so that I can help you become empowered to change your own life.

I've been there. I listen. I understand. Most importantly, I know what it took for me to make strong roots, and with years of hard work and determination, to grow a wonderful trunk and a beautiful, flourishing tree—one that actually has sprouts. And guess what? My "sprouts" (and by that I mean my blessed children) have healthy roots. You have the power to change your future and help guide the next generation, too. I did!

Are you invested in your future? Let's go! I'm right here with you.

YOUR TREE OF LIFE

My healthy, crazy, curvy tree, doing its own thing!
My Tree of Life is growing in a very fun and unique way and having a blast thriving, just like
I am. I surely can't wait to see and hear what your healthy Tree of Life will look like.
Get your journal
Out and get ready to reflect and write.

> You have to expect things of yourself before you can do them.
>
> —Michael Jordan, NBA Basketball star player

CHAPTER TWO

Dream Big

> *I have a dream.*
>
> —Martin Luther King, Jr., Activist, humanitarian

What are your dreams? Come on—start small and simple, and then we'll get to the big stuff. Does a nice, peaceful night's sleep sound great? Write it down. How about spending more fun time with your friends and family? Perhaps take time to think about what would make you really happy and whole, by going for a nice long drive or walk in the woods.

Being coached is action oriented, so you'll want to have a private notebook or workbook with you. Carry one with you everywhere in case you come across great ideas to write down. It could happen at any time.

Let's think of potential goals in your life right now:
- a more balanced school life
- becoming a better communicator

- finishing high school
- striving to achieve all you can so you can get into a good college
- changing habits

This part of the process is "preparing the soil," making sure you're getting your location perfect for you to set down your roots. Also think about when you dig in the soil. It's a form of discovery, isn't it? Well, look at this step as a time to "dig deep" and become open to any ideas that pop in. They may be new ideas about what you want to study in college. You may want to "weed out" certain people in your life that are not that healthy for you and may damage your roots.

Open your horizons all throughout this process and be creative. It's your beautiful life—Your Tree of Life! Look all around you for inspiration—you'll love the process.

Think about and write down where you want your tree to be:
- in the forest?
- by a brook?
- on a lake?
- at a family camp?
- by the ocean?
- secluded on a mountain?

It's up to you. That's the fun of it.

So back to nurturing the soil (sounds like nurturing the soul hmmm…)—we need to make sure the ground is healthy. You don't want to plant it in a toxic place. Now I say these things and use analogies because as teens you're very bright. If you get this right the first time—wow!—won't life be so much easier? I mention toxic because you wouldn't want to plant a tree in a toxic place. It's the same thing as planting it with toxic people. Does that make sense?

Let me explain. I grew up in my forest of toxicity. Many of my friends did similar things that I did—gave up on school (I did for a period of time), and skipped school (I did that, too). Who is that toxic to? *You!* It kills your roots—weakening your tree.

But you can change. I did. That's the great thing. Even if your family is toxic, we'll have tools to use to deal with difficult people in a *healthy* way. Trust

YOUR TREE OF LIFE

me when I tell you, not everyone in the world wants to grow and learn and improve. So you'll always have difficult people to deal with. Together, we'll learn coping tools to have in Your Life's Toolbox.

So we find a healthy place—a peaceful place—with no toxicity, with water nearby, and with healthy soil to get us started.

Now let's get digging. When you start to dig deep, do you think, "Uh oh," or "Hmmm, maybe we'll discover something cool?" A little of both?

When my friend put an addition on her house, she found old bottles from decades ago while digging in the ground under her home. She found real treasures, as she was preparing for her home project. Ponder that when you're preparing your personal soil. For instance, you might think:

- "I thought I wanted to go in the service, but I may want to wait a bit;"
- "I was planning on going straight to college, but my dad was a marine and that would make me proud to also serve my country;"
- "I may try a higher-level class next year;"
- "A tutor would really help me improve my grades;"
- "My friend is really toxic and mean, but I'm a great person;"
- "I'm going to talk with my parents more and really consider their opinions;"
- "Sleep is very important to me;"
- "I'm going to treat my body well and exercise every day;" or
- "I'm too young for a serious relationship—I need to focus on strengthening my roots."

Do these comments and suggestions stimulate ideas for you? I hope so.

As we set up the soil and you prepare your location, you'll see your life improve and you'll feel better about yourself and the opportunities that will become attainable. It's still hard work, but real fun because it's all about you. Y.O.U. You're special. Never forget that!

Look at the picture below, and write in your journal what inspires you about it. Does it give you some ideas about where you want Your Tree of Life to be? Ponder who you'd like to have with you—or definitely not go with you—and don't forget, write in your private journal. You can also e-mail me; I'd love to hear your progress. It's fun and exciting, isn't it?

DREAM BIG

Perhaps Your Tree of Life is on a lake with mountain views and lots of healthy friends to hang out with. Write your thoughts, or perhaps take pictures of some ideas. Share them with friends, or even email them to me.

CHAPTER THREE

Be Yourself

> *I believe there is one crucial element to living a life of joy—being authentic! Many people never learn the lesson and live in the shadows of themselves. Don't let that be you.*
>
> —Alicia Aho

One of the most important aspects of the Your Tree of Life program is being yourself. As we prepare the soil in the perfect location, you need to do some reflection: "Who am I anyway?" Silly question? Absolutely not! Some people go through their whole lives either trying to be someone or something they aren't, or never figuring out who they really are.

How do you find out who you are? There are many ways. However, let's start here: Think about your passions. What that means isn't relationship based but what you love to do. What are you really interested in, and would do well at because it suits your personality? Write down some ideas.

What leisure activities do you enjoy or get passionate about? Start there.

- Do you enjoy working alone, with people, or in groups?
- Are you a team player?
- Are you a family person?
- Do you enjoy family gatherings, outings, or games?

BE YOURSELF

- Do you like being creative?
- Do you get a thrill out of working through problems?

These are all great questions to help you become more self-aware. Thinking about them will also help you to see how you interact with people.

Now, when you're with your current friends

- do you act like your true self, not caring what others think;
- do you change who you really are to meet what you think others would want you to be;
- are you true to your beliefs;
- are you strong in your values and not afraid to stay on track; or
- Do you stray easily from your values with peer pressure to do drugs, drink, and act differently than you know you should?

These are imperative questions for you to ask yourself and to ponder. I'll tell you a little story to show what can happen if you don't:

A very outgoing guy gave my friend the impression that "he was always trying to be someone he wasn't" (her words). He drank too much and boasted about it. He was a great person, but he did wild things that didn't seem to match his character. He had older brothers who were tough and in the military. We don't know that much about his family, but he did plan to go into the military after college. My friend stayed away from him because she's a young person strong in values and convictions and really looks for similar people to be in her circle of friends. However, she was his acquaintance. This young man bought a fast motorcycle, and during his first year owning it—he crashed it and died.

I'm sharing this story with you because I don't want you to be anything but true to yourself. The consequences are steep—sometimes irreversible. *Your life is in your hands. Take the journey, dig deep, and dream!* Discover who you are. Your Tree of Life will be strong. I assure you.

You won't change overnight. I'm famous for saying, *Take baby steps*. Through this journey we call life you'll change many times. You'll add friends, change friends, and experience career moves. You may love a career, get promoted, change companies—make new friends, get a degree, perhaps get married and have a family. Undoubtedly, you'll lose people you love along the way. All of these important parts of your journey are much easier if you're living an authentic life.

So be true to yourself. This book is written for and all about *you*. Work with me as I work with you. You're perfect! Just keep growing—like Your Tree of Life.

> *Be yourself, or you're living a lie.*
>
> —Alicia Aho

BE YOURSELF

How happy is this tree? Definitely has an 80s hairdo. What do you think? Write it in your journal. Actually, all the photos are meant to be part of your action items... to get you to reflect on how you feel about them and what they "say" or mean to you.

CHAPTER FOUR

Your Circumstances Don't Define You

> *No pessimist ever discovered the secrets of the stars, or sailed to an uncharted land, or opened a new heaven to the horizon of the spirit.*
>
> —Helen Keller, 1880-1968 - Deaf and Blind American writer and scholar

    The product of a broken, dysfunctional, abusive, alcoholic home, my family tree was not doing so well, and neither was I.

    When I was in middle school, I planned to go to college and expected to attend the prestigious Groton School, a prep school where my dad worked. (former President Franklin D. Roosevelt went there.) I had the grades required to be accepted; however, my mother objected to my attending because members of my family wouldn't have the same opportunity. That is one of the reasons for the beginning of my decline, my search for a different group of friends, and a means to escape the craziness going on in my house. I almost gave up. I almost changed the person I was (Chapter Three) and became the person others wanted me to be (doing things that weren't good for me or my future). Previously, my grades had been great, but they began to slip.

YOUR CIRCUMSTANCES DON'T DEFINE YOU

I had tremendous responsibility for a preteen and teenager, and the stress was unimaginable. Without the opportunity at Groton, I just began to give up and give into peer pressure. I did have great friends, but we made poor choices. Most lived in chaotic situations like me and coped like I did with alcohol, substances, and skipping school and classes. Needless to say, my constant appearance on the Honor Roll disappeared.

A few years later, after running away for three weeks because I couldn't handle the stress any longer, I gave up and gave in. My mom was going to make me a ward of the state (a foster child). I was a sophomore. I was letting my circumstances define the outcome of my life. It was a lousy place to be. I wasn't authentically me. I was numb.

To make a long story short, a family member stepped in and said, "I'll take you in, but you'll get straight As, go to school, not skip school, or classes, not get into trouble and not party. You have to move tomorrow." I kept to the rules, and I realized at that point that *never, ever in my life would I again let my circumstances determine the outcome of my life.* That's my original quote, and I truly feel they are words I live by every day.

I basically became a walking, talking "middle finger" the size of New York to anyone who said I wouldn't amount to anything (which, unfortunately, in my dysfunctional family, was a lot of close family). My hard work was shown on the honor roll for the rest of my time in high school, and I also graduated from college with an honors gold tassel. I proved to *myself* that no matter what, I didn't need to prove to anyone but *me* that I could be a success. Make sure you understand how important that is. Your success will matter someday to your husband or wife and your children…but make it matter first to *you*, and you can't help but be a success.

So whatever your circumstances are, big or small, don't let them determine whether you'll give up on your own future—especially in America! You have so many opportunities to flourish and grow here. Be determined to be a success.

If you're poor, you can get scholarships, and there are lots of programs to help you get jobs. If you have a sick parent, seek support. Talk to a guidance counselor or a teacher you trust. Perhaps you have a learning disability. Don't be shy about it—get help. There are so many things the schools can do to help you. Just never give up—no matter what circumstances or challenges you have to overcome. You're a success! Believe in yourself. Hey, you're reading this book, aren't you? So you're investing in your future already. Good for you. Now, believe that I believe in you, because I do!

This is part of making strong roots that'll be nourished with healthy decisions—support, love, and hard work. It's just the beginning, but do you have an idea of how this is going to work? Envision Your Tree of Life—your fantastic, unique tree that you'll work on for your whole life. Your tree, your choices—healthy or not, growing or stifled, nurtured or wilted; we'll work on making your tree hearty enough to handle life's challenges!

> Give the world the best you have and the best will come back to you.
>
> —*Madeline Bridges*
> *American Poet (1844-1920)*

YOUR CIRCUMSTANCES DON'T DEFINE YOU

My friend, I love this tree—it says so much to me!
What ideas do you get from this picture? Are your ideas related to my story in this
chapter or related to something in your life. Take a walk or go to a favorite place to ponder
and jot your thoughts down. I can't wait to hear how you're doing with this book!

CHAPTER FIVE

Character and Self-Awareness

> Character is like a tree and reputation like a shadow.
> The shadow is what we think of it;
> the tree is the real thing.
>
> —Abe Lincoln, 16th American President

CHARACTER AND SELF-AWARENESS

Have you ever heard people saying, "I really don't know who I am?" or, "My friend doesn't show her true self." If you take the time now to build your character and become self aware, the gifts will be priceless.

Let's look at some definitions, because I feel these are misunderstood words, and yet, so very important.

<u>Character</u>: "The concept of character can imply a variety of attributes, including the existence *or lack of* virtues, such as integrity, courage, fortitude, honesty, and loyalty, or of good behaviors or habits" (Wikipedia, emphasis mine).

As you read that, do you want to *build* your character to include many of those attributes? That is the start of developing self-awareness. Let's look at that one.

<u>Self-awareness</u>: "An awareness of one's own personality or individuality" (*Merriam-Webster*).

Let's take a look at your character. Really ponder these questions:
- Do you feel you're an honest person?
- Are you generous?
- Do you like to be kind to other people?
- When no one's looking, are you truthful and kind to yourself and others?

These are ways to build your character. Trust me when I tell you building your character to be the best "you" you can be, my friend, this is a gift you'll keep opening every day of your life. As Abraham Lincoln said, "The shadow is what we think of it; the tree is the real thing." If you have integrity and are self-aware, there shouldn't be a big difference!

Teens are among the best people in the world to coach, in my experience. You take the action items and do the work. To benefit from this chapter, you really need to use your journal and write down some of your characteristics. Over the next week, pay attention to how much you let your true character come out. Or do you keep it inside? Then write down why. Is it fear? Fear of what? Fear that people might know you're bright? Honest? Giving? Tough? Give it a shot.

If you worry that people will read your private work, get a lock on it except when you—and only you—are working in it. If you start writing things down, you can start to make your dreams—your true identity—a reality. You can also put your fears down and give them less power. Whoa. Yes, less power! You're powerful.

Building strong character traits (strengths) are very powerful roots to help stabilize your tree. Here are some things to think about regarding your character traits of honesty and integrity.

- When you shake hands with someone, do you look the person in the eye?
- Do you have a firm grip without being forceful or limp? Make sure you have a solid, strong handshake, not a flimsy one. This applies to both males and females.
- Is your handshake your word, a bond, like in the old days? Do you want it to be?

Guys and gals alike—your word builds your character. *Honesty is a large root in your Tree of Life!*

When you look at these bullet points, my friend, what traits do they make you think of? *Stop right now and write down your ideas*—below, in the margin, or in your journal.

For instance, let's consider the first bullet—when you shake hands, do you look the person in the eye? There are many character traits (strengths) that come to mind for me. Let's see if our answers are similar: Looking someone in the eye shows confidence. Take time now to write in your journal your own reasons why you would look someone in the eye when shaking hands. Another idea to write down is if it is difficult for you to look in someone's eye, journal why that is. Never forget, this is a growing process for you. Doing processes like these always help you to become more self-aware. Your Tree of Life is growing! I'm so proud of you.

Second bullet—Have a firm handshake to go along with looking your friend (new or old) in the eye. This is imperative. Practice, practice, practice. When I coach in school, this is taught and practiced; it's *that* important! What character trait would a weak handshake show? It could reflect that you're

CHARACTER AND SELF-AWARENESS

willing to give your power over to the other person. I know that sounds harsh, but this is an important topic. I've met presidents of corporations, people in powerful positions, and shaken hands with "strong" people—some with flimsy handshakes and some with strong ones. I trust a person more if he or she has a strong handshake. I make it a very important beginning lesson with students of all ages, and I don't assume an older or successful person has a strong handshake—I'll work on this with anyone. My friend, I have a disease that munches on the small bones of my hands, and many people in my situation stop shaking hands. But no way…not me! Never forget how powerful you are; and ways you can show that to others in your first impression!

Add to this list. What else can you think of? Write down everything you can think of. Think of people you admire. Maybe they have characteristics you'd love to emulate. Commit to it, my friend; you can and will.

This is an important chapter, but one that you'll refer back to—because no one is perfect. If you're aware of your great qualities and also not afraid to look at areas you want and need to change—whoa—you'll go places, my friend! Self-awareness as a teen? You'll blow adults' minds!

Seriously, many adults don't even take the time to look at themselves and make changes. You probably know many people like that, don't you? Think of them now. Do you want to stay stuck like them? Or do you want to soar? I already see you soaring!

All right, use your journal and get writing. The roots of your tree are your qualities that help your tree grow strong and healthy. You're on your way!

> *It's our attitude in life that determines life's attitude toward us.*
>
> —*Earl Nightingale*
> *American author and motivational speaker;*
> *known as "The Dean of Personal Development" (Wikipedia)*

YOUR TREE OF LIFE

My friend, I have photographed many trees, but this tree struck me as having tremendous character. What do you think? Take some pictures and share them with friends or family…even me. What an exciting journey you're on.

CHAPTER SIX

Discovery

Growing is a key for survival—for babies, plants, businesses, and Your Tree of Life...also known as *you*.

Last chapter, I spoke about your character and how it's one of the strongest roots in Your Tree of Life. Now we need to reflect on and journalize your traits. What are your traits that you want to grow? Don't forget, my friend, as long as you're healthy and making positive decisions and having fun...who

DISCOVERY

cares if you grow differently than your friends? Right? It's *Your* Tree of Life. This apple tree looks like she's having a blast!

On that note—as this is a journey, and life is about personal awareness, growth, and discovering who you are, what do you want to do with this gift we've called life? Where do you begin? The best place to start is to uncover your *passions*—the things you love to do. Stop right now and write in your journal or in the margins of this book. What makes you smile? What do you love to participate in? Having this information in front of you as a list to keep adding to may help paint a picture of where you want to focus your attention on in college, or in your job search, or in future classes. Most importantly, in this self-reflection, it is a way to find the way for you be happy in your life. I hope that makes sense.

Here are some ideas:
- Music
- Sports
- Acting
- Debating
- Writing
- Driving
- Learning
- Drawing
- The sciences
- Traveling

I could go on and on, but that should give you a start. Personally, I love to read. I always have. You'd find me walking to the library, two miles from home, as a ten-year-old clutching my pocket dictionary (which I still have), and I'd check out as many books as I could carry. I've also been a life long learner. Some teachers and many other careers need people with this desire. Participating in sports shows a discipline, as does playing an instrument; your willingness to practice and keep advancing and learning on your own. I was in a drum and bugle corps and twirled a rifle for years. That took tremendous practice and patience. I see how my interests in and outside of my school years molded me in my careers, without me really even knowing it. Imagine how much further ahead you will be having this knowledge

YOUR TREE OF LIFE

I'm talking about your passions—and how you can turn them into a life or a career. For me, being an avid reader and a lover of music, I evolved into a writer at a young age. First it was poetry, then my life story, blogs, and now this book. These passions strengthen my roots. It took a long time for me to get to this point in my life. Also, during my careers, I was able to utilize my passions in various ways, and when I was able to be with people, and write and create, well, that makes me the happiest. Sometimes, along the way, you may not have the perfect situation, but never forget the list we are talking about and you are creating. Go back to it, add to it, and use it throughout your life for school, sports, college, and work. I hope, with your reading my books, your journey will be gentler, more efficient and organized, and quicker—so you can begin living your dream! That's my goal for you.

Also, my friend, explore the qualities you have. Are you outgoing? A perfectionist? Are you shy, sometimes afraid to ask for help? Guess what—all types of people need guidance. You might think, "What would an outgoing perfectionist need help with?" Perhaps more than you'd expect. In high school, college, or even in the workforce, we all have to learn when and how to communicate best with our peers. Sometimes it's hard for outgoing people (like me) to *not* communicate. And on the other hand, if you're shy and need to ask for help in order to grow, you just have to do it. If you're ever unsure, ask a clarifying question—whether it's in high school, college or in the work environment. Even if you pull someone aside to do it—it actually shows you're action oriented and that you care. You'll be thankful later. Trust me—I've been the "brave one" asking the questions my whole life.

I worked in the pharmaceutical industry for many years. We were constantly tested, and passing required a 90 percent minimum on each pharmaceutical subject we studied. I needed to know my facts, so I asked—sometimes many different times to different people—until I finally "got it." You know when algebra just clicked? Or physics? Or trig? Or calculus? *To grow you must know—and to know requires no fear of asking.*

In this chapter, reflect and look forward to the following questions:
- What has made you the happiest?
- What comes to you naturally?
- Where are you the most comfortable?

DISCOVERY

These questions will give you clues to help you on your journey. Go to a special place—the woods, by the water, at the library, in your room, etc.— to contemplate and write down your discoveries. It's Your Tree of Life.

> What lies behind us, and what lies before us,
> are tiny matters compared to what lies within us.
>
> —*Ralph Waldo Emerson (1803-1882)*
> *An American Poet & Lecturer*

CHAPTER SEVEN

Strengthen and name Your Roots

What type of learner are you?
- Are you a <u>visual learner</u> (someone who needs to see a problem displayed to grasp the concept)?
- Maybe you're an <u>auditory learner</u> (someone who relies on hearing, as you would in a lecture or listening to recordings).
- You may be a <u>tactile learner</u> (feeling what you're learning by touch)?

I like to coach with all three methods. It is a great life lesson to know how you learn best as well.

As I have mentioned previously, becoming self-aware is a great gift.

STRENGTHEN AND NAME YOUR ROOTS

Notice anything about these roots? Your roots are all over the place. That's how a healthy tree grows—with lots of roots. Think about it. When you're walking in the woods (which I hope this book is inspiring you to do), you trip over roots all the time. Now imagine your Tree of Life, your roots. What are they going to represent in your life? We are going to spend a few chapters on this. It's key to creating a strong core for Your Tree of Life.

When I coach this Your Tree of Life curriculum in high schools, the roots take several weeks of reflection. Let's see why. Your roots represent what you need to strengthen you. Everyone's trees will have some of the same roots but also some different roots. Let's look at some examples, and then you'll have some time for journaling.

When you think about life, you need basics. Are you getting them? Take a few moments now to think about self-care:

- Do you eat well? Do you have healthy meals, perhaps even together with friends or family? Look up healthy meals, and you can find lots of great recipes for everything you're looking for. Should that be one of the roots on your Tree of Life? Write it down. It's OK if you're not sure—use a pencil for now.
- How about drinking water? Do you drink the recommended eight glasses of water a day? Well, let's get moving in the right direction… what do you say? Sound good?
- Do you exercise? If so, do you do it on a regular basis, making a positive difference on your well-being and your cardiovascular system…as well as your muscles?
- Do you get enough sleep? One hundred percent of the kids I coach don't get enough sleep or sleep way too much. So, would healthy sleeping habits be good to have on your roots?

Let's investigate that. Are you one of those who doesn't get enough sleep? I recommend to my clients to get at least seven hours of sleep (good, solid sleep) per night. How many quality hours of sleep are you getting? How does it affect you? If you don't get enough sleep, do you notice a difference? The students I coached who made sleeping a priority for themselves got along better with others, could focus in class, didn't fall asleep in class, and improved by whole letter grades. Imagine that! All by making sleep a priority. Yes, put sleep/rest on a root! Definitely. For the rest of your life. You'll thank me for it, trust me.

All of these are so very important, my friend. Don't forget; we have but one life to live. <u>Homework</u>: Take a walk in the woods and look at trees. Notice the trees or sprouts that are healthy, well nourished, caring for themselves. You'll also see some that are broken, rotted, fallen over, and weak. Which one do you want to be? If you live in an urban area, perhaps you can go to a park, or even look for beautiful pictures online.

So we have healthy eating, plenty of drinking water, and adequate sleep. That's a great start! Oh yeah, and exercise. Let's talk about that root some more, too. That will really make Your Tree of Life strong. I believe your generation has so many great opportunities to find a perfect way to stay fit—and love doing it.

I'm going to list some of my ideas, but first, right now—stop. Pick up your journal and write down physical activities you now enjoy doing alone or with friends or would like to start/learn. See you back in a few.

Now, back to my list:
- Running
- Walking
- Yoga
- Dancing
- Biking
- Aerobics
- Swimming
- Tai Chi
- Pilates
- Working out at the gym
- Hiking
- Walking your dog
- Rugby
- Exercise shows on TV

STRENGTHEN AND NAME YOUR ROOTS

- Weightlifting
- Boxing
- Team sports
- Stretching

Phew, that's tiring work, but worth it. Wait until you begin being the great caretaker of you, nurturing your roots. Create a strong core. Whoa—you'll flourish, my friend.

Now, when you're thinking about your sleeping routine, I've heard and seen it all. I, myself, am a horribly light sleeper, and I need so much help to get a good night's sleep, but I do what I have to. Right now—write down in your journal how many hours you're sleeping per night and what actions you'll take to change that. You may need to turn off your phone when you go to bed. It can be a huge distraction. If your phone is your alarm (one of the girls I coached figured this one out on her own)—buy an alarm clock. White noise is great to drown out others' voices. I use a fan. (OK, I use *two* to help me sleep.) Some alarm clocks have really cool sounds on them like birds, crickets and waves crashing. Dark blinds are good. A new pillow only costs ten to thirty dollars, so if you need a new one, it's a wise investment. If yours has been round since you were six, maybe your parents will swing for it. Going to bed at the same time every day and getting up at the same time (within an hour) is very good for your body. We all need seven to nine hours of sleep.

You may already have great habits—continue them. Or you may need to first identify healthy ways to live, ways to change. And then, my friend, with effort, support, and care for yourself—you'll thrive!

To summarize this chapter's action items, we are working on your roots. As I mentioned earlier, this will be something we'll work on for a few chapters, taking our time on several individual roots. This is because change takes time. They say changing a habit takes twenty-one days. Twenty-one days to have your new change become part of your lifestyle. That's what this is about—changing your way of thinking and doing it one baby step at a time.

So back to the action items (AIs). Do you remember them? Stop. Write down what you think they are. There are only three for this week's chapter:

- Take steps to improve your sleep routine.
- Eat healthy. Make it a lifelong change. Have it just be who you are and what you eat. (No four letter words in my life: D-I-E-T? No way!)
- Drink lots of water. That's an easy one. It's inexpensive, and you'll immediately feel and look better than if you've been drinking sugary drinks or alcohol instead. Buy a nice water bottle—a really cool one—and keep it filled all day long. Trust me on this one.

That's it for this week's AIs. Don't forget, these are just ideas. But to get Your Tree of Life to be the best one on the block, near the ocean, in the forest—wherever you want to have Your Tree of Life to be—to have it be healthy and strong, it all starts with roots.

> *Make a habit of reading something inspiring and cheerful just before going to sleep.*
>
> —H. Jackson Brown Jr., *American Author*

CHAPTER EIGHT

Habits
Strengthening your Roots

> We are what we repeatedly do. Excellence, then, is not an act but a habit.
>
> —Aristotle (c. 384 BC – 322 BC)
> Ancient Greek philosopher

To me, good habits are a way of life, in a ritualistic way. Like getting up, making your bed, then brushing your teeth, putting on your makeup (if you choose to), and finally cleaning up the bathroom counter when you're finished.

Now, my friend, I'm not perfect. Actually, I have to be more ritualistic because I have a disease that's eating away at my joints, and every day I have stiffness, pain, and fatigue. Every day for me is like having the flu. I really need good habits to keep my own house clean because I wouldn't have the energy to clean it if I didn't.

So when I say habits are a way of life—I mean it! People also make poor habits a way of life…and an excuse! For instance, not cleaning up after yourself or sleeping the day away instead of trying to create a positive habit or two are poor habits many of us have dealt with at one time. I'm telling you right now—I don't buy it. You *can* change. Life is precious. It's short, and you need

STRENGTHENING YOUR ROOTS

to respect yourself and the people around you enough to create and keep good habits for a lifetime. Imagine good habits for a lifetime. Imagine the example you, teenagers of the world, will make on others when you begin living today—thriving with good, clean, healthy habits. Once you start with clean surroundings, your mind is free to expand and explore all the world has to offer you.

I truly believe a cluttered room leads to a cluttered mind. Now many people may disagree. However, if you get your space clean and make a habit of keeping it clean, I bet you'll have less anxiety about situations. I even venture to guess you'll sleep better in a bed with clean sheets. You may even want to have friends over when things are all cleaned up.

Now, here are some ideas for new habits you might like to create:
- Clean out your backpack every week.
- Do your chores without being asked.
- Wash, dry, fold, and put away your laundry.
- Have an organized closet.
- Organize your binders.
- Purge your e-mails periodically.
- Make a birthday calendar and send cards. (This is a beautiful habit, especially sending cards via mail.)
- Make a regular habit of taking care of your pets. (Bet you said you would a long time ago if they bought you that puppy.)

As the last chapter said—make habits of:
- sleeping well
- eating healthily
- drinking water (try to drink six to eight eight-ounce glasses)
- exercising—(try for at least three to five days a week) but it has to be one you love to do or you won't make it a habit.

To summarize, this chapter is about strengthening your roots. It's about setting daily habits that you engage as soon as you wake up and continue all day.

These simple small changes will make a world of difference. Your room will be clean, because it stays clean. Your schoolwork will be easy to access because you made a habit that worked for you to stay organized, even to the point of having your parents buy you a new binder, or whatever you envision working best with the way you learn and organize. Now that you're really taking the time and making an effort to get your life in order, people will see the changes and will help you. You'll see.

I recommend buying a laundry separator. Perhaps this is something else you can get your parents to help you with. Trust me, as a mom, if my kids were getting organized and asked for a laundry organizer so they could take better care of their rooms, I'd take them on a shopping spree.

As we all know, habits take time to make into "just the way you are." Twenty-one days straight, I say to you, my friend—go for it. Take baby steps. It's up to you to embrace your life and the quality of life you want. Together, let's create great habits, personalized for you—ones that will make you feel proud, make your life easier, and help you to thrive. This will allow you to make time for the truly fun stuff—living life!

STRENGTHENING YOUR ROOTS

One of my habits to maintain my health is to walk on these beautiful paths! Now, my friend, you get to see the trail I walk on that helps inspire me, and bring me joy. What are the habits that bring you joy?

CHAPTER NINE

You Control Your Future

> *Cherish your dreams, as they are the children of your soul, the blueprints of your ultimate achievements.*
>
> —Napoleon Hill, (1883-1970), American author and writer of many works related to personal success.

As you read about Your Tree of Life and building strong roots…some of them go together, don't they? Like habits—those encompass a lot of "roots" to strengthen them. However, as your coach, I also need to provide you with tools along the way to make these changes. Otherwise, they are just names of roots.

YOU CONTROL YOUR FUTURE

After three years of coaching students at one of the largest schools in New Hampshire, I was amazed and captivated by the ability of my students to set and achieve goals! These weren't small goals either. These were sometimes life-changing goals to put their lives back on track. Some students committed to quitting smoking cigarettes, stop fighting at school, making positive life changes, participating more in school, and many more amazing achievements.

What was the difference between other people asking (or telling them, begging them, threatening grounding if it wasn't done) those teens to do these things and with their working with me in my Teens Empowered Coaching Program? The answer was as individual as each and every one of those students, just as you are. They became accountable to themselves for their own growth and worked hard to make changes that would affect the rest of their lives. And you can be as determined as them to decide the outcome of your life. You. Y.O.U.

That was what happened in a class setting. Can it happen with a book? Absolutely! I'll help you, but it's up to you. You have to make a commitment to your future and decide the outcome of your life. You're in control.

When you hold this book in your hands, know that it's like looking at a path with two turns. One is the easy way—the other way is your best life's destination. For this, you have to take action.

YOUR TREE OF LIFE

The big decision—the easy way...or your best life's destination? Choose right, my friend, and your life will be full of joy and richness—not wealth necessarily, but happiness to go after your dreams and to work hard! I'm so very proud of you!

Never forget, my friend, even if you choose the easy way—if you make a decision to do nothing—you're still making a decision. Make the right decision for today and for *your future*. It doesn't matter what's going on in your life—bad, horrible, stressful, unsupportive environments, etc.—at this stage of your life, you're responsible for the success or failure of your life. So choose to succeed. It's your life to live, not anyone else's. Am I right?

YOU CONTROL YOUR FUTURE

You control your future, your destiny. What you think about comes about. By recording your goals and dreams on paper, you set in motion the process of becoming the person you most want to be. Put your future in good hands—your own!

—Mark Victor Hansen, *Author of many books, including Chicken Soup for the Soul*

CHAPTER TEN

Making Changes

> *Nothing changes if nothing changes.*
>
> —Unknown

As teenagers, you're changing all the time, but are you consciously making the decisions to make those changes? If so, are they good decisions, taking you in positive directions?

I'll be specific about both making changes and how to know when, and if, you should change something. See this tree above? It's changing—with the seasons. Sometimes it's good for all of us to reflect and make appropriate changes every time we go from spring to summer or fall to winter…and now you have your trusty little journal to reflect on your growth and see where you were, where you are, what changed, and what changes you still want to make. Perhaps shed your vibrant old leaves and get a fresh new set in the spring after really working on yourself in the winter. Hmmm.

    First of all, what do you do that gives you peace of mind? What clears your head? Taking walks? Running with an iPod? Fishing? Going to a park and sitting on a favorite bench? Sitting in your yard in your favorite chair with music? Driving?

    I want to make sure that when you need "you time," precious time to process life's situations, you know where to go and what to do—the places and actions that make you feel better. As I write this, I'm having "me time" after my mom passed away. I knew what I needed to do, and I'm doing it—with support, of course. For me, right now, I am away looking at one of my favorite lakes, staying right on the lake in a lovely little lake home with a porch and deck on the lake with chairs. This environment not only comforts me while grasping this sad time, but also enables me to put pen to paper and compose not just for you, but other works as well. Poetry is another form of writing for me.

    Here, as I am making changes in my life, living without the loving support of my mother, I have to first grieve, and yet, at the same time, live. Here, on Newfound Lake, my family found a lovely place that provided a location with great opportunities for walking, so I am able to exercise, but also clear my mind. Being an approachable gal, I made a friend and while alone here during the week, she is coming over for dinner, and we also walk together. This most important time in my life to make a change has been made manageable, and comfortable due to my self-awareness, and tremendous support. Hopefully, through sharing my difficult time, it will provide you good understanding of the importance of making changes, and also to have tools and support (friends, family) ready for when something difficult happens.

    So let's look at making changes/choices and figuring out how to go about that the best way:

    <u>Friends</u>—Let's say you're hanging around with friends who are beginning to do drugs or treat other people in a way that isn't true to who you are. You have a choice to make, right? You could stay friends with them but not hang out with them exclusively. Perhaps you could choose to quit drugs if

you've started using them (and get support for that) and surround yourself with healthy people. I know these choices are often harder than they seem. However, your future relies on the great decisions you make *now*. There are kids just like you, who you can befriend—without drugs, or alcohol and bad behavior. Trust me. As you grow older, you'll realize that life isn't a high school popularity contest. Far from it.

<u>Colleges</u>—See guidance counselors. Go to college fairs. If your parents help, great. If not, it doesn't mean you can't go. Just put one foot in front of the other. Perhaps find a mentor teacher to help you get there. Teachers love that, and you'll know who to ask. I'll talk more about mentors in chapter eleven. Research colleges and while running, walking, meditating, etc. evaluate your options before/or after journaling. Never forget, you can change majors and add minors to your degree program. You can even decide to go to a totally different school. If you keep your heart and mind open, your dreams will come to you. The first year of college is good for getting core classes down and figuring out where and what you want to study. Just keep moving forward, my friend.

<u>Contemplate your dream career</u>— What can you envision yourself doing? Have you already volunteered and loved it? Or do you have no clue? Have you read books with characters in them that have fascinating careers that interest you? Or perhaps you are researching careers? Job shadowing is a great idea too.

Making changes is a powerful subject in your life, and if you learn young, to develop healthy ways for you to contemplate your choices, you'll trust your decisions more, without that "woulda, shoulda, coulda" feeling. That's why I write this for my young (and not so young) friends—so you eliminate the mistakes and the time it took many other people older than you to figure it out.

So go get comfy somewhere and reflect on what decisions you have going on. Write your thoughts down in your journal, even—pros and cons—and revisit your list in a day or two with a fresh mind. Trust me, life whizzes by, but you'll have the time to reflect and make good decisions. It's always your choice—make it a good one!

MAKING CHANGES

My mom's tree of eternal life! When my mom passed away, I went away to take care of my soul—and this is the tree that I was blessed to look at every day. Can you believe the tree and view that was placed in front of me as I took the time to reflect and make changes? What special things have "shown up" during hard times for you? Write these in your journal.

CHAPTER ELEVEN

Find a Mentor or Two

Look at these two! One is the mentor and one is the teenager who is being taken under the wing of his/her very talented, trusting role model. What does this picture say to you? Write it in your journal. After this chapter, get ideas about who you'd like to ask to be your mentor...or where you're going to go to seek one.

FIND A MENTOR OR TWO

Hello, my friend, let's talk about mentors. Wiktionary defines a mentor as, "(noun) a wise and trusted counselor or teacher." As you grow and determine where your life is going to take you, it's always great to have people on your team.

Now you may say, "I have my parents." Great. "My boyfriend or girlfriend is very supportive." That's fine, too. The kind of support I'm referring to is from a trusted teacher, guidance counselor, perhaps an adult family friend you respect and admire, or possibly your boss. (My former manager is a great friend and mentor of mine and has been for over fifteen years.) Know that you can use your family as mentors as well, if they are willing to take on that role.

There are so many people in your life, but as the definition states, a mentor is "a *wise* and *trusted*" person in your life. It's helpful if this person (or people) knows you pretty well and is willing to spend some time with you to take you under his or her wing. Sometimes, having a mentor just seems like an extension of a friendship, but then you ask the questions you save for them. For instance:

- What do you think about this job?
- Where do you feel I could improve the most, and how would you do it?
- I'm thinking about going to this college. Can I run the pros and cons by you over coffee?
- What are five things I could do today that you did to make a difference in your life?
- What are some good resources (books, audio books, online classes, podcasts, etc.) that you'd recommend to me?

You get the idea. If you're willing to find a mentor (or two or three), you must be willing to consider his or her (or their) advice. Are you?

This is another area where your tree is gaining strength. Roots are getting solidified…because you're doing the work. You should continue to work with mentors during your whole life and eventually become a mentor to someone else. It will be a life changer, and Your Tree of Life will be so strong because of it.

> *Teaching kids to count is fine, but teaching them what counts is best.*
>
> —Bob Talbert, Journalist

CHAPTER TWELVE

Surround Yourself with Trusted Friendships

> We have committed the Golden Rule to memory; let us now commit it to life.
>
> —Edwin Markham, *American poet*

As I go on my daily walk, I'm always looking at the forest to tell me its story. I get it. It's perfect, especially for a chapter about surrounding yourself with trusted friends you can lean on. As I was walking the other day, I saw a tree that had broken in half and was being held up by its neighbor—midair. Everywhere there are trees leaning on each other. Some grow up together.

SURROUND YOURSELF WITH TRUSTED FRIENDSHIPS

Some lean on each other as they mature. Sometimes the branches reach out and permanently hold up their friends. Don't you want to have a friend like that? Me, too!

I can't express enough how important the word "trusted" is, when it sits before the word "friend." There may be many friends who come and go in your life, especially in this Facebook age, but how many of them can you really truly trust? How many friends would carry you over the long haul? You might be surprised at the number. As time goes on, if you can count on your hand(s) a number of true, trusted friends who've been there throughout your life—consider yourself blessed.

You may ask, "Why do you dedicate a whole chapter to this?" It's so important to have people in your life—friends and family—to share your joys, your struggles, and the daily blessings of life. You never know what hand life will deal you, and if you have a few trusted friends to lean on, and they can lean on you, well, you're a lucky person—you both are fortunate.

Don't be surprised if, when your beautiful Tree of Life starts to grow and blossom, some of your friends fall away. You may never know why. Just keep growing. Never stop growing. There are plenty of other Trees in the forest!

Never give up. Be bright, kind, and bold, and always give back to others. The Golden Rule - "Do to others what you would want them to do to you" is simple, an "oldie but goodie." Use this rule as your way of life, and you'll always have trusted friends because you'll be one.

Take a few moments to think about your closest friends. Do you give more than you get? Are you a taker—more of a one-way friendship? As with anything in life—you *can* improve. You can *learn* how to be a better friend. Life also is a great teacher on unhealthy relationships, so evaluate yours. Make sure your friendships are healthy and growing, and most importantly, that they don't stop your growth. Great friends should and will encourage your growth.

I've been dealing with being ill for many years. For a couple of years, it was hard to focus on reading a book or watching a movie or having a conversation. I never gave up on my dreams, and my doctors never gave up on making me better or helping me accept my reality. I also have a friend who I asked to coach me when I was diagnosed with Rheumatoid Arthritis, a systemic autoimmune disease where your body's cells attack itself. Every day I have pain in my joints, severe fatigue and sometimes, while my disease is very active, it has begun to erode (eat away) at joints in my hands. The medicine I have to take really weakens my immune system, as it is my immune system that is attacking my body. The medicine makes me more vulnerable to colds, flus, bronchitis,

SURROUND YOURSELF WITH TRUSTED FRIENDSHIPS

pneumonia, west nile virus…etc. Recently, I have been diagnosed with at least one more autoimmune disease, but once you have one, you are prone to getting more. Not good for a hardworking personality like me. Deb, my coach/friend recently recognized, when I was feeling sorry for myself, that it took losing everything for me to actually achieve my dreams! It takes bold, honest friends to tell you the truth, but you need to surround yourself with people like that. It has been her friendship, support and love, as well and reminding me what I can still do, when I may feel like it isn't close to as much as I used to. Friendship is awesome.

Remember, it's not about how many friends you have. Life isn't a popularity contest. You don't need superficial people. You want friends with deep roots and strong convictions who will stand for something—even if it's alone. You want friends who will stick with you, strong or weak, rich or poor, climbing the ladder to the top. None of that should matter to a trusted friend.

A trusted friend is someone who lets you lean on him or her when you're feeling weak, laughs with you after you've shed some tears, and accepts you as you are, as you grow and change over the years. That's my kind of friend.

CHAPTER THIRTEEN
Use Resources to Help You Grow— Personally and Professionally

We had a violent thunderstorm here last night. Whoa, it kept me up. However, on my walk today, the trees seemed happier. (Yes, I said it.) There were more birds chirping, and I'm looking at a beautiful heron right now.

> They don't care how much you know until they know how much you care.
>
> —President Theodore Roosevelt, 26th President of the United States

USE RESOURCES TO HELP YOU GROW...

New creeks, brooks and streams were flowing, and the roots of the trees and vegetation were getting nourishment. It was nice to see a few new faces— the heron and some birds I haven't seen around here before. We needed the rain. The birds, animals, and the area needed the important resource; water. Without this resource, we could have a drought.

We all need to nourish our souls, our minds, and our lives like this. Without learning, education, reading, personal growth, Your Tree of Life will wither away. You don't want that. No way.

Whatever direction your life takes you, never stop learning. How do you keep your tree watered? One example is to read! Always read. Another example is to research. You know I have given many other resources in prior chapters, but this one will focus on reading and researching.

Here is a compiled list of examples of both:
- Read for pleasure, but for every pleasure book, have one or two more books going that related to your current or future career interest.
Read stories with lead characters in positions that you're interested in (either nonfiction or fiction), and read the history of the book if possible depending on the book. There may be enough information

for you to keep notes. Always keep adding notes in your Moleskine or notebook. You may decide, during your research, (consider this a nutrient in the water), that what previously seemed very interesting may have you completely changing courses, per se. That's why research is *so* important. Where reading may be the water in Your Tree of Life, researching can be the nutrients from the water and the soil that continues to help your tree gain strength. Just as reading and researching are making you a strong, self-aware human being. Another great way to learn is online through classes called webinars. There are many classes that are free. This is a popular new way of learning/researching. For instance, the *Harvard Business Review* has great articles, blogs, and webinars, if you or your parents subscribe to the magazine. I'm sure, looking online, you'd be able to find many articles, blogs, and webinars related to many different fields. I am sure there are local classes you could take online or in person to gain more insight. Perhaps your parents, or you, may be able to speak to a guidance counselor to see if they may print out articles that may be pertinent to your passions and interests. Read them—forward them if they may be relevant for a classmate or colleague. It will be appreciated and shows your initiative.

- Look at magazines that interest you; there will be many. The more diverse information you house in your brilliant mind, the greater the opportunities that await you. There are magazines/articles/books on nearly every type of career you can think of…or perhaps you never thought of, until you read about it.
- Online, my friends, there are blogs and articles written by professionals and passionate people who love what they write about, for instance - photography. If you love photography and would love to get more information on "how to", look online, for any topic, and you will be amazed and thrilled at how much help is out there! I'd love to hear from you and what you learned about!

My friend, I assure you, I spend a lot of time doing work related to this chapter, and I will for the rest of my life. These are ways for you to strengthen your roots and the core of Your Tree of Life. How exciting! Take this seriously.

USE RESOURCES TO HELP YOU GROW...

Ponder where you feel you should begin and go for it. Jump in with both feet. It's just expanding your knowledge base and becoming an expert in your field. Doesn't that sound fantastic? Get started. Your Tree of Life is looking for new streams to sustain it.

What are some of the resources you use? How do you use them and where do you find them? Is this chapter helping you discover new ideas?

CHAPTER FOURTEEN

Important Roots to Nurture as Well as Exploring New Branches

> Love not what you are but what you may become.
>
> —Miguel de Cervantes, 1547-1616, Spanish Writer

IMPORTANT ROOTS TO NURTURE AS WELL AS...

It's time to take a look at your strengths. My friend, the next couple of chapters are ones that you'll want to put aside time to truly reflect upon.

In this day and age, there are so many opportunities for you to take your strengths and passions (Chapter Fifteen) and create your own brand new ideas. Sprouts are all around us in the forest. It's the same with ideas, there are never ending ideas you can come up with for your future, and I hope this book is a good guide. Your tree can have many branches that represent things you have learned; many of your experiences are both life and work related, and related to you branching out to college, and so much more. Keep your eyes open to all that you do and experience and write, write, write, in your journal. This will help you organize your journey, and I will explain more later as far as other ways to utilize the information you gather during this process.

The world is becoming smaller and smaller, isn't it? That means more opportunities to share your strengths and passions.

What are your strengths? Start with what comes naturally to you:

- Are you a self-starter?
- Are you great with your hands (working on cars, repairing things, designing)?
- Do you work well with people?
- Would you be that big, strong tree in the forest others would lean on?
- Do you like to talk with others?

Is reading a pleasure to you? If so, what you read may lead you to your passions. Keep your eyes and ears open. You're in the exploring phase. This is fun. Really.

Speaking of exploring, this is such an important phase of your discovery. Take time for this. Go for a walk or a bike ride, but whatever you do, bring your journal and reflect on your strengths—write them down. Think back over your life and just keep writing or recording—you could record it in your phone.

Another way is to ask your parents, your "supporters," and your friends that you would you feel comfortable asking: "What do you view as my top three strengths?" Don't give them any hints. If they need a "for instance," provide them one of their own. How does that sound? The more you have, the fuller your leaves in your Tree of Life will be. Do you know why? It's because, one, you asked for help, and two, you received it.

I would repeat this process for your passions and facets of your character you would want feedback about! That, my friend, is a strength—asking for help.

IMPORTANT ROOTS TO NURTURE AS WELL...

My friend, ponder over your feedback. Are you surprised? Happy? Is it helping you move forward on your journey? I hope so. Jot down how you feel, and make sure you don't lose the positive feedback. It'll be a treasure. Trust me. Even if it's your own thoughts—those are priceless, too.

CHAPTER FIFTEEN

What Are Your Passions? What Brings You Joy? What Will Bring the Blossoms out of Your Tree of Life?

Find a job you love and you never have to work a day in your life.
—*Confucius*

WHAT ARE YOUR PASSIONS? WHAT BRINGS YOU JOY?...

My friend, this quote represents the core of your happiness throughout your long life. Becoming self-aware, through this book, and throughout your life by following the simple, yet not easy work here, you will be able to have great joy, and success. In your free time, what do you love to do? Is that a skill you could develop by going to college or applying for an apprenticeship?

Here's an example that has presented itself to me as I'm writing. I just asked the young woman sitting next to me, Rachel, the question, "Are you passionate about what you're doing?" Here's what she told me: She has a bachelor's degree and has worked in Human Resources, had another management position, and bartended. These positions didn't bring her joy. Guess what she's doing now. Taking a test online before she heads to a college nearby to work toward a manicurist license. After that she'll need six hundred hours of apprenticing at a salon for manicuring. Guess why she's doing this. Passion! Joy! She loves the social interaction of the career, and one of her strengths (Chapter Fourteen) is being an artist. Rachel loves drawing.

Joy! Every day of your life you need it—you deserve it. Go out and get it. Find it. You're never too young or too old to discover your true path. It's never too late, my friend.

Not sure where to start? Think through your life. When have you been the happiest?:

- Were you in a group setting?
- Were you a leader?
- Did playing an instrument bring you a smile?
- Were you in a marching band?
- Were you playing on a team or individual sport?
- Do you enjoy meeting new people?
- Were you speaking in public or to new people or would you rather just quietly keep to yourself?
- Do you love animals?
- Have you been happy while gardening, either growing flowers or vegetables?

All of these are more clues to add to the prior chapters to put pieces together so your life will be more fulfilling and you won't waste precious time doing other positions that don't bring you happiness.

We are here but for a short time. I strive to assist everyone I coach in making his or her journey easier, more joyous, and peaceful. Don't you want to do the same? Begin today. Reflect, write, and reflect some more. Talk to your friends. Ask them what they think brings out the joy in you. Where are you the happiest? What are you doing? It's not going to come to you overnight, my friend, but if you don't move forward, where are you going?

For instance, I was speaking with a nineteen-year-old student—let's call him John—who wants to play hockey at a good college. That's his joy, his passion. It's also the passion of others on his team. However, John also realizes that in order to achieve his hockey dream he can't sit at home with this buddies and not take classes. He needs to "feed his brain." For John, he needs to not just play hockey, but also understands his brain thrives on learning. He knows that life is a balance—to achieve and receive the blessings of our joy, we have to work hard to get there. In John's case he needs to balance his passion of sports with his passionate pursuit of his career. He doesn't take it for granted that although he is a very talented athlete; he needs to also get an education to enable him to pursue a career that he will love. Way to go, John.

Some of us experience joy at home as parents—as caretakers of our homes. That's awesome, too. Since I became ill, I've lost careers and my ability to work in the capacity I was previously used to. This situation strengthened My Tree of Life because I discovered my purpose and I'm achieving it.

My joy was and still is and always will be around my family. I'm blessed now that, with my circumstances, I'm always here for my family. That is a blessing.

WHAT ARE YOUR PASSIONS? WHAT BRINGS YOU JOY?...

Another blossoming Tree of Life full of joy!

If you truly say to yourself, "I've always wanted to...," "I'm happiest when..." write that down. Those are branches of your tree. You need to go out on a limb and explore. Will it bring you joy? Or will the branch break off? Visualize your thoughts and write or even draw your conclusions or ideas. I can't wait to hear about it

> *Blessed are the joy makers.*
>
> —Nathaniel Parker Willis
> *American Author, Poet and editor*

CHAPTER SIXTEEN
What Are Your Nonnegotiables?

Your Tree of Life might like to be around a family camp on a lake. You may, too!

> It's good to play, and you must keep in practice.
>
> —Jerry Seinfeld, Actor, comedian, writer and producer

My friend, life is meant to be lived, and live we must. Your Tree of Life is meant to grow strong deep roots, a wide trunk, and many beautiful branches of diverse experiences, passions, and strengths.

WHAT ARE YOUR NONNEGOTIABLES?

Now this chapter is a seriously fun one. Get out your journal, and let's get writing and pondering. These nonnegotiables—things you won't give up, no matter what—give more character to Your Tree of Life. Can you imagine why?

If you live away from home and put on your list of nonnegotiables "Sunday family dinners," it can really solidify your support of your family, as well as your family becoming more like friends for you. As a mom who has family time with kids who no longer live at home, I can tell you it would mean the world to your family and hopefully to you and eventually to your partner. That's one example. I hope that help clarifies a little what I mean.

Here in New England it's getting warmer, so my fiancé and I went for a couple of walks with friends (well, we picked them up along the way—isn't that what's fun about being sociable and living in a neighborhood?). That's a nonnegotiable for me. I have to do a workout of some sort every day to keep my body healthy and not freezing up. I modify every day. That's another example.

Take some time now and truly think back over the last twenty-four hours. What did you do that was very important to you, that you wouldn't want to give up? Of course, you already know I would suggest you put exercise on the list. Find one you love! Lord knows if there isn't something you could do for half an hour a day, well, I'd be pretty disappointed, but I'd still care for you just the same.

All right, how about personal time? That's so important now, when it seems like every second people are tugging at your time. I find walking on the trails "right sizes" me. Plus, you know, the trees tell me their stories. Put a chair and a couple of books in your car so you can stop if you see a great spot like a lake, a view of a mountain, bottom of a trail…go for a stroll then have some quiet time to reflect. Always bring your private journal book we've been using for this journey! If there are no trails locally, you can always find a park, or when I lived in the city, I always enjoyed walking or riding my bike in the neighborhoods.

Do you have hobbies or things you'd love to do but never made time for? Now is the time. Perhaps you're a collector, but your collection is in a shambles—now you can get it organized and make it a showcase. How about being an unprofessional anything. A photographer? Print out photos and put them up. Again, showcase your work. Perhaps you draw or paint? Get started. Do you play an instrument? Go for it. Are you social and want to plan "game night" with neighbors but are a little reluctant to ask? Just do it. You'll have a blast.

Many cultures have lots of family time. I wouldn't call it nonnegotiable, as it's just how it is. I recall when my children played soccer there were families from Nigeria every day playing bocce and smoking cigars. I bet that was a daily nonnegotiable.

My fiancé, Derek, is British American, and I love Saturday mornings with him because when we aren't running around, we watch proper British *footie* (soccer). The fans are so into the game. I also enjoy when we are able to catch a rugby game. Derek played rugby in school growing up in England for many years, and finds leagues to still play when he can. When his parents move here, I can't wait to learn more proper British family-time experiences like "high tea."

In our family, we write each other notes—mostly Derek and I to each other, but we also write them to the kids. Before our bathroom got painted some of the post it notes we wrote landed on the walls of their bathroom. Our kids have said they loved to read them. Even if it wasn't said outloud…the post-its stayed up for over a year - with dozens and dozens of notes for everyone. I think they liked them. So a little gesture of gratitude to my whole family, every day, in some way—be it a note or a hug or even a smile and a thank you—is a nonnegotiable for me. It's all good, isn't it? Hey thanks for taking the time to work on you. It's good work, and you're worth every second.

WHAT ARE YOUR NONNEGOTIABLES?

Another idea of a nonnegotiable—perhaps you love the water and want to spend more time there, regularly. Write it down. While you are contemplating ideas, keep writing them down, Adding anything you love and will not give up that adds joy or meaning to your life.

CHAPTER SEVENTEEN

Education Is a Strong Root to Help Your Tree of Life Grow

> *Read books! Read books! Read books!*
>
> —Herman Wouk, Pulitzer Prize Winning Novelist

As I write this most important chapter, I reflect to my Teens Empowered classes. What fun! What an inspiration those teenagers were to me. I was coaching freshman to seniors at a local high school. Some had plans to go to college and did. That was great. Today, my friend, even more so than when I was in high school—many moons ago—further education is so important.

What I'd like to discuss in this chapter is, what is it you really want to study? How do you best learn? You have so many more subjects to choose from compared to when I was your age. You may be a hands-on person who enjoys cars or equipment. Try to get an apprenticeship. Some high schools also let you begin taking classes (even tech) related to your dream career. Make sure you take advantage of what you can, my friend.

Many colleges offer two-year associate and four-year bachelor degree programs. Even if you plan to get a bachelor's or even a master's degree, I urge you get the associate's degree first and keep moving forward without a bump in the road. Why, you ask? I know many people that say, "I have no degree even though I went to college for three years," or, "I'm three courses from my bachelor's degree, but I have nothing to show for it"? Life happens to all of us. If something happens in year three of your college career, you have an Associate Degree and are working on a Bachelor Degree. Plus, it won't look bad to have an associate's, a bachelor's, and a master's. Right?

So back to what choices you have to make. There are online courses you can take. I even take free webinars all the time from well-known authors; business leaders, etc.….make sure you keep learning, even if you already have a degree—or three.

If you decide to go to an online college—make sure you do your homework to find out that it's accredited. Be very careful and check referrals and past graduates.

To help you figure out what direction to go, check out what tools your school has. Go see guidance—they'll point you in the right direction. Not only that, but I know they have tests that help lead you into certain fields based on your skills. They give you quite a few career choices based on your skills, if I recall, and you can ponder that, too. This is your wonderful, beautiful life's entire story. You get to fill in the blanks. Just really do it well, my friend.

Trust me, as you'll see with trees, our lives' paths never travel in straight directions—many have curves, changes that happen. For instance, as I mentioned in Chapter One, I was on my own at sixteen. Well, being so young and in a "survival mode," not a teenager having fun, enjoying life, and my grand choices, I didn't have many choices at all. I had to find work, find transportation (from about twenty miles away), go to school, get good grades, and get accepted into a college in a different state because I was moving. Whoa! My Tree of Life was, at the time, at the growth stage. Thank goodness for friends and the aware teachers, including at Bay State Jobs for America's Graduates, who helped me.

The jobs I'd had up to that point and classes that I'd done well in were business related—especially accounting. I actually worked for the city auditor for at least one summer for Neighborhood Youth Corp (a summer job program for poor kids). My point in sharing all this background is so you understand why I went to college for accounting. I was in "survival mode" for many years (that's for another book), so I did what came easy for me: accounting.

I did what I recommend as well—I received an AS in accounting, on Dean's List. And then I went to school at night for a total of eleven years—all while buying a home, having two babies, and maintain a full-time accounting career. I also have my BS in accounting, on Dean's List, too.

Another way to get your education is to find a company to pay for your tuition. You can find out if they offer that by looking at the benefits package. Sometimes it will be listed in the ad for the position. I'll tell you, it's difficult, but perhaps you could go for your associate's and find a company to pay for your bachelor's. Or you could get your bachelor's and get someone to pay for your master's.

Additionally, after figuring out what you want to study, then look into where. Schools have many different ways of teaching and also specialize in particular programs. For instance, a private school in Boston specializes in teaching and social work. It also is primarily a writing school (no formal written tests). If teaching or social work is your passion and tests are difficult for you, this school may work for you. These are things to look into when the colleges come to your school or you make a visit. So very important, don't you think?

To end the chapter, I'd like to remind you that college is expensive no matter where you go and you're required to pay your loans back. Even bankruptcy doesn't relieve you of them. That is why I encourage getting assistance such as a company paid tuition. See Fastweb.com, where there are lots of scholarships to apply for. The one thing I'll say about going to Fastweb.com, your guidance counselor, or a college to apply for scholarships is: follow through. Give it your best effort. Won't it really be a nice thing to begin your life after college with minimal debt? It sure will.

I hope this chapter was helpful and made you do some writing in your journal, especially keeping track of colleges you are thinking of, career or degree ideas and any information you have gathered. I know reading this chapter is making your life stronger because you're planning your future, which is one of the ways to nourish your tree. Good for you!

EDUCATION IS A STRONG ROOT TO HELP YOUR...

One of the reasons I came up with Your Tree of Life is education. Many families feel stuck if, for generations, no one went to college. Perhaps your family situation is in abject poverty, like mine was. If you have inner drive, you're bright, and you want to go to college but fear it will never happen, it will! You've already been making strong roots with that inner drive, studying, reading, and hoping. This chapter will help.

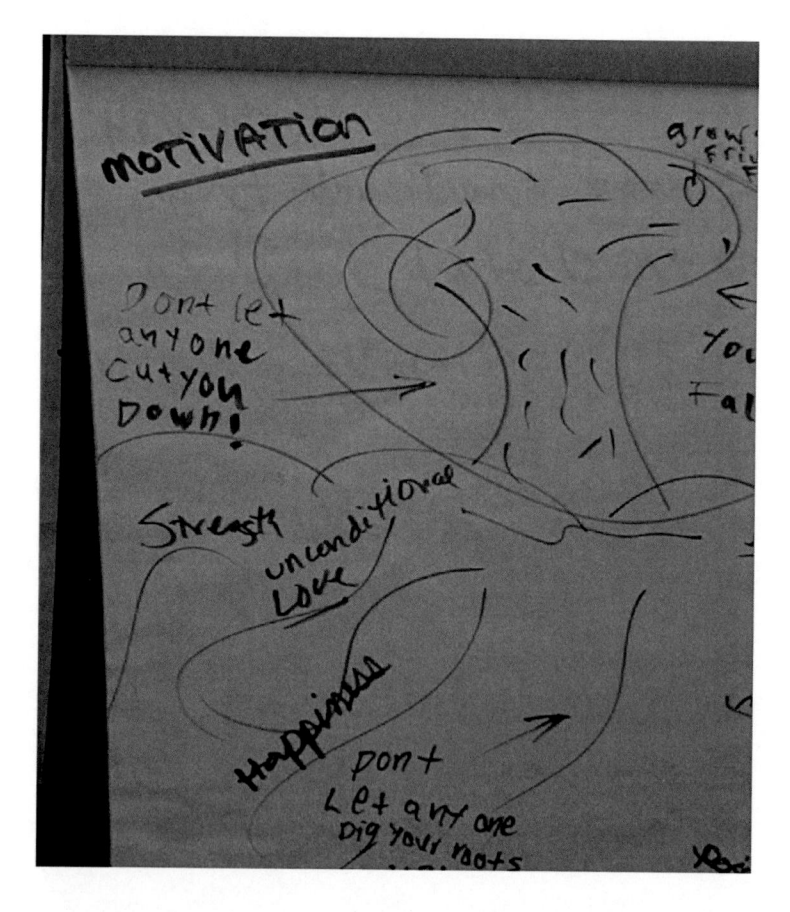

One of my flip chart pages—to display some high school students' Your Tree of Life process. One of the roots, not in the photo, is education. You can see the creativity already going on here. The students' interpretation is awesome to behold. I can't wait until you delve into your personal growth.

CHAPTER EIGHTEEN

Playtime: Everyone Needs It— Your Tree of Life Needs It, Too, Like Water and Air

> Laughter is the shortest distance between two people.
>
> —*Victor Borge, Danish comedian, conductor and pianist*

Playtime! I think of the trees rustling in the breeze and kids playing hide and seek—hiding behind trees, rocks, bushes. "Ten, nine, eight, seven, six…"

"Hurry, hide over here."

"Shhhh!"

"…five, four, three…"

"Ahhhh."

"Shush. He'll find us!"

"…two, one. Ready or not, here I come!"

Oh, what fun it must be from a *branch*'s eye view of the craziness of kids playing. Do you remember riding your bike with complete freedom?! I loved riding my bike everywhere, right up until I couldn't ride it anymore…but I still have my bike, because I plan on getting better, and playing on my bike again!

PLAYTIME: EVERYONE NEEDS IT...

I digress. Think about the fun things you love to do with your friends now... and what you used to do when you were younger and had a real free spirit! Never lose that spirit!

Climbing trees was another favorite pastime of mine as a kid. Yes, I was quite a tomboy and a tough kid. I could climb right to the top, too. Oh, we had such great trees—and tree climbers. I was so grateful when my daughter went right for our tree and began to climb it when she was (kind of) old enough.

My practice for Drum and Bugle Corp or gymnastics just became part of playing outside. I carried my rifle everywhere, as I was in the color guard. To become a better gymnast, I would cartwheel myself wherever, do backbends, handstands...you get the gist. That only stopped when my shoulder got operated on much later in life. Even in my thirties, when I got a sale when I worked in advertising, I would do a cartwheel in the radio station offices. I was known for this—crazy and full of spirit! I was nourishing my soul. However, having an autoimmune disease eating away at my body was beginning to eat away at my spirit...do you know why? It was taking away my playtime! And so it was taking away who I was, who I really was at my core.

Life happens to all of us. Sometimes it even happens when you're a teen. I just felt I needed to tell you this because now, *writing for you* is my playtime. I can't wait for this book to hopefully inspire many of you to make changes, especially if it's playtime! Put down those videogames and play board games. Play games that have you looking at and interacting with your family and friends. Go out and play. Ride a bike. Climb a tree. Play Frisbee. Throw a football (I taught my kids how to throw a spiral in the good ol' days). Play catch! Make up your own family games or friend games. Why not? No rules in my book.

Spend time walking on trails and just listen to the rustling of the leaves, the crunching under your feet, the wind in your face. Feel the sun on you—it's wonderful. Find places like that near you and go often. You'll be getting exercise without even feeling like you did!

Call some friends and get a pickup game of anything: basketball, softball, baseball, soccer, rugby, football—it's all good. Maybe have a barbecue after or a potluck—that's the best.

Perhaps you're saying you're too young to plan all that. That's OK. Ask your parents—perhaps they're friends with your friends' parents, too. I know I was friends with my kids' friends' moms and dads! If they're not, don't worry. Just play—enjoy every day. Life will all figure itself out if you keep making the right choices.

Remember things you did for play that were emulating what your parents or other role models did? For instance, did you make mud pies and decorate them and then have a party…using mom's tools and scrap wood to create? I made tons of things with my parents' tools. The best was a bed/TV tray for my mom I built out of wood and leftover bathroom tiles. I always leaned toward being a carpenter—I was tough, but this was playtime. Did you do things like that? The best part was you were playing, learning, growing, and then *giving*.

How about playing strategic games with soldiers or cops and robbers. How fun! My fiancé Derek's dad just dug up his garden and found a soldier of Derek's from thirty-five or so years ago. Imagine that.

Some other ideas are fishing. Do you enjoy fishing? It can be such a fun experience with awesome memories. Even if you come up flat, it can still be a fun day on the water. My Memere and I would get up before dawn with flashlights and buckets. Do you know why? We were night crawling. We would get the worms as they peeked up to the light on the fresh morning dew. It was so much fun, and of course *extremely* competitive. Then we would go fishing with my Pepere, sometimes in his 1927 T, bucket crank-up car. How cool. I can't wait to hear your stories.

Dancing, singing, swimming, farming, fixing cars, car racing, horseback riding, dog walks, going to the beach, skiing/snowboarding, reading (find a cool spot), rollerblading, acting, going to plays, writing…

My friend, this was a fun chapter to write. I hope it was fun to read. Hopefully, you stopped and took time to reflect along the way and wrote in your journal about ways you look forward to incorporating into your playtime, and fun memories of joyful playing that made you smile. Playtime is so freeing, but how you play also may lead to how you live, how you determine your strengths and passions. If you're lucky enough, you may be able to do a job

PLAYTIME: EVERYONE NEEDS IT...

that's like playtime. So, my friend, back to your playtime to keep nourishing Your Tree of Life and most importantly, you. You're growing in such a healthy way. You have more tools in Your Life's Toolbox now.

This tree is having fun! What do you think? Looks like joy to me.
"Laughing deeply is living deeply."
—Milan Kundera, Novelist

CHAPTER NINETEEN

Areas You'd Like to Improve to Strengthen Your Tree of Life

> *Real integrity is doing the right thing, knowing that nobody's going to know whether you did it or not!*
>
> —Oprah Winfrey, Philanthropist, talk show host, media Proprietor

My friend, nobody is perfect—especially me. I try to reflect daily to see where I could make changes to make life easier, make myself kinder, etc.... You see where my thoughts are; now let's see where my pen takes me.

When I speak about ways or areas of improvement or time to reflect on perhaps some deep changes, I mean ones that could right-size Your Tree of Life.

When I was a young teen—believe it or not—my friends and I faced similar stresses to the ones you and your friends face now. In this example, I'm referring to body size. This has been a battle my whole life. Now, my friend, trust me, enjoy your teenage life—if you're doing what we already talked about—eating healthier, exercising, sleeping seven to eight hours a night—you're golden!

At a young age I was tiny—four foot eleven, almost a hundred pounds. When I hit a hundred pounds, something shifted in my thinking and I believe

AREAS YOU'D LIKE TO IMPROVE TO STRENGTHEN...

went into a bout of anorexia. I ate hardly anything at all. I weighed myself every day. I got down to eighty-nine pounds, and when I visited a family member, he was astonished. He forced me to eat while I was there, as I was afraid if I didn't. When I went back to non-eating, at the time, my sick mind thought, *Luckily, I didn't gain weight*. Eventually, I went back to a normal eating pattern; however, at that time, we were very poor so we didn't have much food. I did have places to go to get food here and there. I'm telling you all: if you find yourself in this situation, talk to someone and get help. You're beautiful or handsome. Believe it!

Something else that I thought would be appropriate in this chapter would be forgiveness. Although you're young, there may be people you have resentment toward. Is it eating you up? Do you know what helps a little bit? Honest forgiveness of the person and what he or she did or didn't do. For example I've had people in my life I've had to forgive for not protecting me. Can you relate?

If you "get it" and this section speaks to you, perhaps writing a letter to the person, reading it out loud alone, and then burning it in a fireplace would be good place to begin healing. When the time is right, when you're older, you can do it face to face, but for now do the letter. By doing this, Your Tree of Life just got stronger and so did you. I couldn't help smiling while writing that part. Forgiveness has been the biggest gift in my life. It has given me so much. However, I wasn't ready for it until my thirties. That's why I coach teens (as well as adults)! Why waste time? I got precious time back with my mom all because of the power of forgiveness.

Are you hard on yourself? "Oh, I should've gotten an A plus, not an A minus," or, "Oh, my project sucks!" But you got an A on it. You're an honor student or a good kid but just so hard on yourself. Knock it off! We have but a short life to live. Accept that you're doing your best (if you are) and then, let it go.

My friend, a great quote for right now just popped up from a book I'm reading, from Willow Creek founder Bill Hybels, and he says, "Most people feel best about themselves when they have given their very best." How true. So reread the above paragraph and this one, too, and if you're doing all you can, smile, breathe, and enjoy life. Keep moving forward toward your dream—as you're doing all you can today.

YOUR TREE OF LIFE

My friend, I wanted to give you a nice peaceful picture for this chapter. This chapter may or may not be a little challenging, but look at how far you've come. Do a lot of self-reflection and of course—write in your journal.

I'm so happy and proud to be part of your journey.

> The truth is that our finest moments are most likely to occur when we are feeling deeply uncomfortable, unhappy or unfulfilled, for it's only in such moments, propelled by our discomfort, that we are likely to step out of our ruts and start searching for truer answers.
>
> —M. Scott Peck, American psychiatrist and author

CHAPTER TWENTY
Always Keep Growing

*This happy 'old chap' surely is a lifelong learner and, I'm sure,
is full of wisdom, joy, and stories.*

    Little seedlings are wonderful to see in spring, aren't they? A sign of renewal, of rebirth, of a fresh new start. I love spring! As I write, it's spring technically in New England, but the seedlings I speak of are only in my imagination…buried under the snow. However, they are there, growing. We all know it. Battling, doing everything the trees have to do to survive and *thrive*…winters, storms, hurricanes, lightning, kids climbing and breaking branches (like I did). Yet, they keep growing. Trees keep growing with *all* of those struggles.

So can we! *Can't we?* Of course. Now, I want you to consider a phrase but not as just a phrase. I need you to consider it as a commitment to yourself. Ready? I want you to be a *lifelong learner*. Whoa. Yup, a lifelong learner—that will surely help Your Tree of Life stand strong and proud in the forest.

What is a "lifelong learner"? My friend, it means always stay interested in life, in the world, in learning about other cultures, perhaps; know what's going on in other businesses beyond the one you're in. Read, read, and read! If you love novels, some novelists add historical truth to the stories in their books. That information can help you learn about some history. Learn about the world's history—there are plenty of videos that can give you excellent synopses of the major events. Definitely know the history of your country! This will help you so much—you never know the people you'll meet.

A beautiful young lady, Emma, was talking with me, and I asked her what she thought about this topic and helping others grow (Chapter Twenty-One). Emma says she always keeps growing by having a healthy lifestyle. She works out five days a week doing martial arts. Whoa! You go, girl. By the way, she has never done drugs or alcohol. That's awesome. Emma also has a mentor (a.k.a., a "believer in you"). Please, my friend, if you don't have one by now, search your soul for who would be a good match, go back to Chapter Eleven, and take action. It *will* make a world of difference to you.

Finally, Emma eats well and is a "perfectionist." Now I don't encourage perfectionism, ever—but I do encourage eating well and having good habits (Chapter Eight), as they are key for your ability to learn and to always keep growing.

I sure miss my walks on my trails—the trees always have so much to tell me. After a long winter, I'm sure they'll have a lot to contribute to how to always keep growing. Funny how the trees tell me their stories, but they do.

Do you have a favorite trail you like to walk on? Or maybe you have a place you like to visit if you live in a location without trails nearby. Perhaps you can go for a stroll or drive and see if you get any ideas while you're out there. Free your mind, bring a small pad and pen and write what comes to you. Just doing that is growth, isn't it?

YOUR TREE OF LIFE

A new idea to think about is your group of friends; do they have the aspirations you do? Perhaps you could begin a book club, reading the new, cool books that are relevant and interesting to people your age, and especially, to you. Alternatively, you could attend classes called Adult ed in some places, that can be anything from painting to dancing; from accounting to basic science classes in some places. Most are offered nights and weekends. These may help you additionally decide what you'd like to do for a career, or study, and/or to add depth to your life. You will also have the opportunity to meet new friends!

You can change your course in life anytime...like this tree!

ALWAYS KEEP GROWING

Truly, this is one of my favorite trees, as I believe it visually speaks volumes about being able to change courses in life...whether changing careers, starting healthy habits, getting out of an unhealthy relationship, beginning the next stage in your education. It's all changing courses in Your Tree of Life...and as your Tree will still grow, this one shows you that it will flourish, too! Reflect on upcoming changes and changes you made throughout this coaching process. Perhaps draw Your Tree of Life as you see it. I'm so proud of you.

CHAPTER TWENTY-ONE

Help Others Grow

> Don't just say how to...show others how to...
>
> —Emma, age 17, NH

Notice anything? One tree is reaching out to help the others, or maybe to show them the way to live without drugs and alcohol and still have fun. What do you see in this picture? Take out your journal and write down your thoughts about this as well as the ideas in the chapter.

HELP OTHERS GROW

You've *certainly* developed over these chapters of coaching and growing. Remember when you were discovering your location and nurturing your soil, all processes of self-discovery and self-awareness? You chose your tree and grew strong roots by hard work on your personal discovery and being willing to make changes where needed.

Your Tree of Life's core became stronger as you became willing to continue this coaching process. It isn't easy, but you're doing it. Whoa, what a fantastic life you'll have. As you were looking in the mirror, this truly was a lesson in self-awareness and shows your character, my friend! You'll go far.

The next chapter will be on your future—but now, let's talk about how *you can assist* your classmates, peers, siblings (perhaps), to grow as you have. Know, though, that not everyone wants to grow. That won't hinder our progress to help others, will it? Why should it? It didn't stop me from starting my idea, turning it into a workshop, and then writing this book. With your help, imagine the healthy, self-aware teens we'll have among us. Whoa, how wonderful!

Imagine truly letting the word out, that *your circumstances don't determine the outcome of your life; your actions and attitudes do.* This is my favorite personal quote, and I'm sure by now you know why—with all of your work on yourself.

I sat next to a seventeen-year-old student Emma (who I spoke about in Chapter 20), a senior now, and asked her about her experiences. She let me know, "As a freshman, I watched healthy seniors that were nice, wholesome, volunteering, and I wanted to *emulate* them." Talk about emotional intelligence for a teenager.

These are some of Emma's recommendations for achieving a healthy Tree of Life:

- Getting a mentor. (We discussed that in Chapter Eight.)
- Going to college
- Taking good care of your body.
- Eating healthily
- Getting good grades
- Never doing drugs or alcohol. Thank you!

Emma made these recommendations because she was helped by others on her way to personal and academic growth. What better way to give you examples than by having it come from someone your age that has walked a similar path that I am hoping you will. In essence, she is one example of helping you grow. Now Emma may or may not get a lot of support at home—I don't know—but she's doing a great job. So are you! As I've always said—one baby step at a time.

Ways to help others grow would be:
- Take them along your walks with you. Why not, right? You'll have company, everyone will benefit, and you'll have fun.
- How about forming a study group? I bet if one person had the courage to start one, it may be a success. If not, perhaps you could just study with a friend.
- Introduce this book to friends who could use it. Let them know how it helped you and that you could be a resource for them if they have questions.
- Be a good listener. That's why we have two ears and one mouth. I always have to remind myself of that. Sometimes, your friends will need someone to listen to them. You get to know one another better, and it can *strengthen* the relationship. (Sometimes you can listen without offering a solution to their problems. That can be difficult for many personality types, mine included. Food for thought.)
- If you haven't recommended the book to a particular friend, you may mention that in this personal coaching book you're working on, there's information on mentors. Perhaps, with your encouragement, your friend may be able to find a mentor to help him or her through a situation (college, moving out, getting a job).

One of the greatest gifts we can give to others is time. You have given yourself so much time, energy and effort for Your Tree of Life...now it is your turn to share your knowledge with others. Don't forget that even sharing a smile with someone is sharing one of life's most precious gifts, being kind.

CHAPTER TWENTY-TWO

Enjoy the Fruit of Your Effort

> *Don't be afraid to go out of a limb.*
> *That's where the fruit is.*
>
> —H. Jackson Browne, author of *Life's Little Instruction Book*

It's Your Tree of Life, my friend, *Your* Tree of your Life! You created it from the idea and then, the ground up. What an exciting journey. I'm thrilled that your tree is flourishing. Sad, too, as I love writing to you, and now this book is almost complete. It's a connection, like our trees are in the same forest hanging out together now, roots intertwining. If you ever need a little help, you can count on me—and the healthy people you've built relationships with along this journey—for some strength and guidance from the roots up. That's enjoying the fruit of you effort!

ENJOY THE FRUIT OF YOUR EFFORT

Also, you know how much effort you put in (as long as you're being honest with yourself. If you're not, no biggie—just go back a bit and build up where you need to—no judgment. Remember, only love and support).

Now, my friend, Your Tree of Life must be standing tall and proud, and even if it's a leaner or a crazy curvy tree—great posture speaks volumes of the confidence you must feel now. Can you feel it? I'm at my usual spot in Panera, on my heating pad, and I can't get the smile off my face. I'm so full of confidence and pride for the healthy choices I know you're going to make. My friend, know also that when faced with tough choices—and you will be every day—*you've built a strong core*. You know who you are!

Do you have any idea, truly, how far ahead of other teens you are? Even college students and adults! The self-awareness tools you have in Your Life's Toolbox are amazing—and you can always look back in this book and in your journal for more guidance.

There are so many great authors out there! I encourage finding genres you enjoy reading and then ask friends or even a librarian or teachers about good authors. Someone I really like for personal growth and leadership advice is John Maxwell. Another great, a writer for *Harvard Business Review* blogs and author of *18 Minutes*, is Peter Bregman. I'm sure with the Internet the way it is, you're already following great writers. If not, try following either one of those two. Maxwell has "A Minute with Maxwell" video each day on his website Johnmaxwell.com, and Bregman has a great blog at least twice a month at Peterbregman.com. I give these resources to you as a great addition to your library, and trust me, these two guys are *gems*. I also know you'll see that both of these gentlemen are authentic, as we discussed in Chapter Three. That, my friend, is very important.

My friend, these tools and resources will help you when those times arise that you may want to move against your core values. Read what these men have to say, have confidence, and use your mentor and the healthy people in your life to help guide you back on track. That's what they're there for, truly. This is part of the fruit of your effort. It's effort to get to the fruit, isn't it? Sometimes it's hard to do the right thing, but it's always the right thing to do.

YOUR TREE OF LIFE

Speaking of the fruit of your effort, did you get accepted at the college of your choice (if you're at that point)? Did you at least make a plan to go to a college that has a program you're passionate about? I sure hope so. What an exciting time for you! If it isn't your time, come back here when it is. Are you feeling your branches reaching out and blossoming as you plan for college or a technical college? I'm so very proud of you. Or perhaps the best way for your tree to grow is by becoming an apprentice, like the girl I mentioned previously in the book who became a manicurist. She has potential to really blossom and purchase her own salon.

You see, my friend, this time can be scary; we all know it's a difficult but an important time. Think of the people who tend apple trees: they work all season, working hard for a great crop, for a sweet apple, to reap the rewards of their efforts. They get joy from our joy of consuming their apples. Imagine reaping the rewards of *your* efforts. This is one of the most exciting and challenging times—keep putting one baby step in front of the other! Just keep moving forward. There's help everywhere. Just ask for it! When you're with finished school, won't that apple taste sweet? Just keep growing—and truly enjoy the rewards of your very hard work, soul searching, and life's changes.

As you continue to grow and watch Your Tree of Life blossom, you get to enjoy the rewards of your extremely hard work, dedication, and tenacity when times got difficult. You get to know that when others gave up and gave in—you didn't. You grew. You grew! Yea, you. Woo hoo.

ENJOY THE FRUIT OF YOUR EFFORT

My friend, what do you consider to be the luscious fruits of your hard work?
You know what to do, grab your notebook and write your thoughts.
Put down the first fruits of your hard work
that come to your mind, and then go back and add more.
Your work is priceless!

CHAPTER TWENTY-THREE

Flourish

> *To be what we are, and to become what we are capable of becoming, is the only end in life.*
>
> —Robert Louis Stevenson, Scottish Novelist, Poet, wrote *Treasure Island* and *Strange Case of Dr. Jekyll and Mr. Hyde*

My friend, five years in the making and here is the last chapter in this book for you. Close your eyes. Visualize the forest in the summer or fall. The trees are flourishing, loaded with beautiful leaves of all shapes and sizes. The wind blows, and you hear the hearty conversations the leaves have with one another. Perhaps you don't have to close your eyes. Maybe you're on a trail and can bear witness to the secrets the trees tell in all their beauty as they flourish. They worked all through winter storms, spring thaw and showers, summer heat, and now they love this time of year.

Sound familiar? You've done the hard work, just like the trees. Do you feel like you're *flourishing*? That you did all you could for Your Tree of Life? As we began with, *your circumstances don't determine the outcome of your life; your attitude and actions do!* You, my friend, are in the last chapter, so you know, *regardless* of the status of your own family tree, Your Tree of Life will flourish!

What do you think? Did it work? I'm smiling ear to ear, still so proud of you. But are you proud of yourself?

Now is the time for you to feel exuberance or perhaps serenity. You may feel joy or peacefulness in the process. My friend, you're on to the next steps, and they're all completely *your* ideas of what flourishing means to you. You know, I'd love for you to keep the healthy habits we established in this book—always—so you'll continue to be healthy.

Now, you can discover what success means to you. What is *your* definition of success—or opinion of success? Flourishing may be the time to pursue a career as well. It doesn't have to be, as it's just the next chapter, but you can always refer back to any chapter in this resource, anytime. I hope you will.

I want to wish you joy, passion, love, challenges to help you grow, support along the way, and—most importantly—success to keep you utilizing your strengths and passions! Make time for your friends, family, yourself. Pursue your hobbies. Read! Truly, keep learning. Look for more of my books. I plan to write and speak a lot. I love to hear how my students' Trees of Life are growing and flourishing. Feel free to email me at teensempowered@icloud.com

Thank you for your dedication to yourself! May it bring bountiful blessings to your future generations, as it will to *you!*

YOUR TREE OF LIFE

My friend, I was taking pictures of fruit, and I came upon a nest. How appropriate this was the very last picture I took. If done properly, you'll have a bountiful Tree of Life—cozy for friends and family to "nest" in and for you to feel authentic and full of joy. You're ready to take on the world!

Made in the USA
San Bernardino, CA
29 May 2015